I've never considered myself as a visual artist, I took classes in school as electives but my portraits seemed more abstract than real with the exception of one subject...the Titanic. When the wreck was discovered in 1985 I used period photographs as reference to draw my first versions of the ship herself. With age comes wisdom plus an added benefit of being friends with maritime artists introduced a more three dimensional effect to my works.

When I wrote "Touched by the Titanic" for the 100th Anniversary I placed copies of the paintings into the manuscript as an extra portion which demonstrated how a child's passion can grow over time. I've been flattered by requests from people asking to see the images produced as a full artbook. With a current Titanic project under production at the time of writing I'm happy to share the artistic impression of a bygone era.

W.E. Brower Jr.

June 2014

TITANIC THE LEGACY REMAINS Artwork

A COLLECTION OF IMAGES PORTRAYING THE

LIFE AND DEMISE OF THE R.M.S. TITANIC

MAY 31, 1911-APRIL 15, 1912

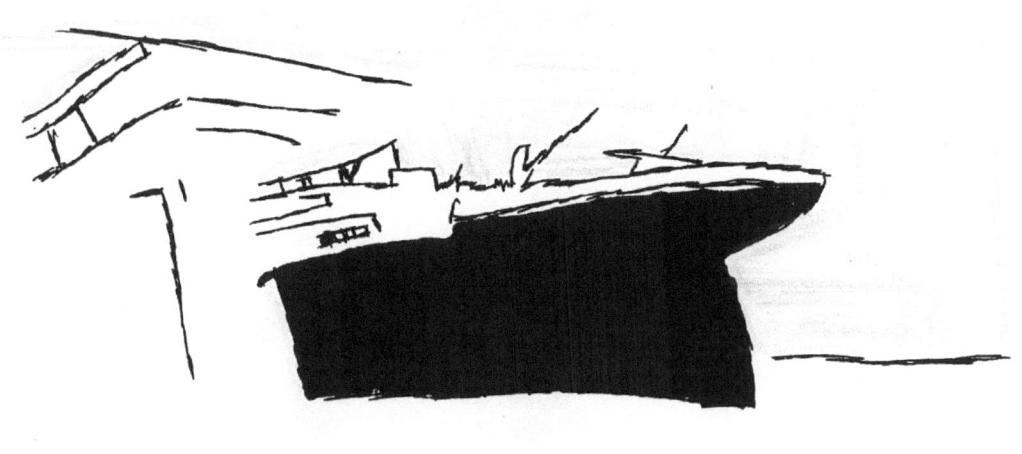

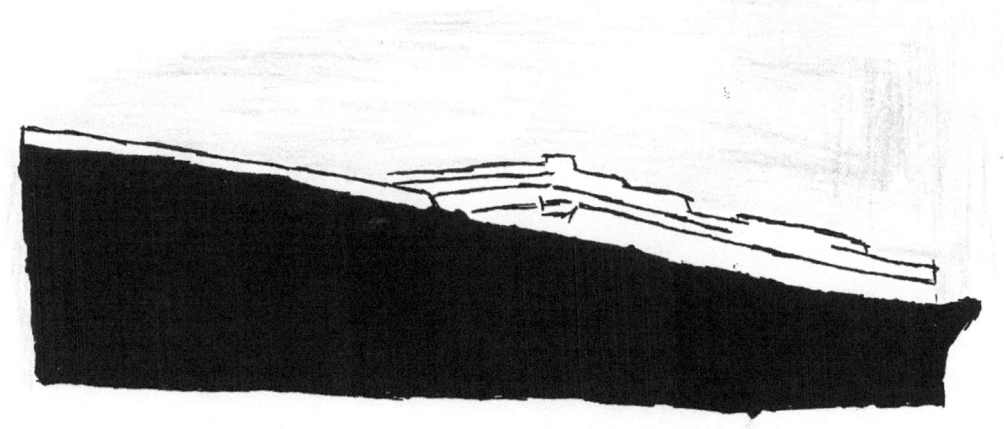

BIRTH OF A LEGEND MAY 31, 1911 TITANIC IS LAUNCHED

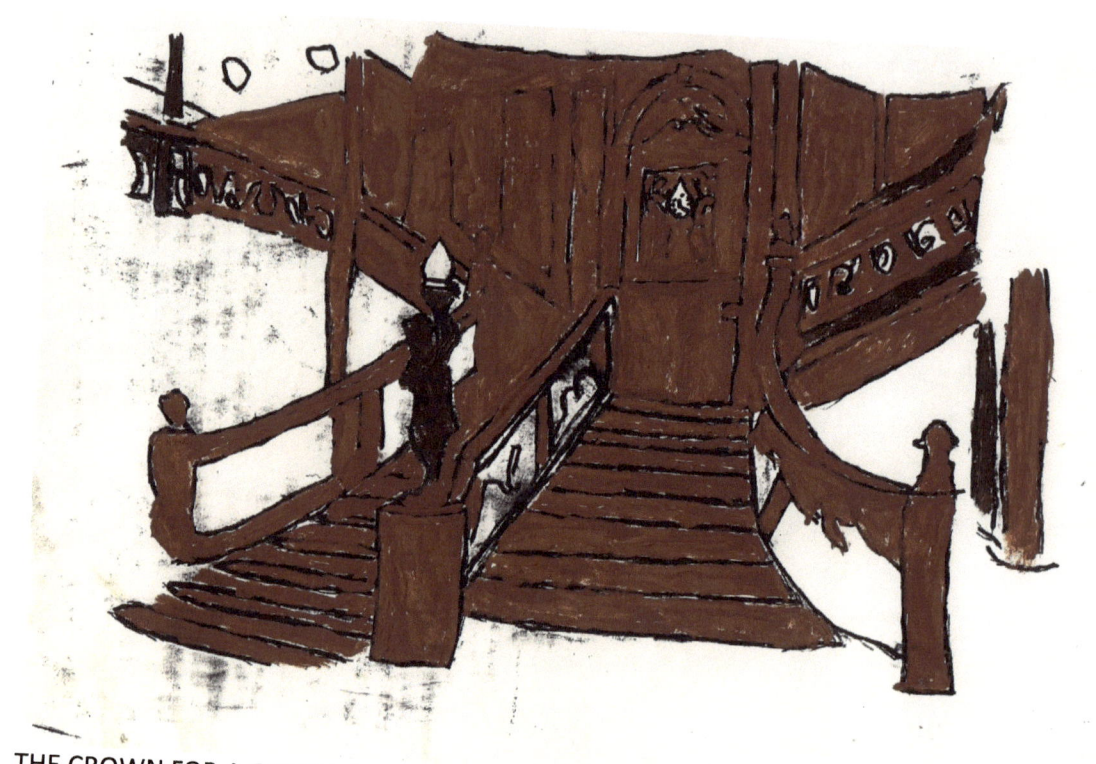

THE CROWN FOR A QUEEN, THE GRAND STAIRCASE

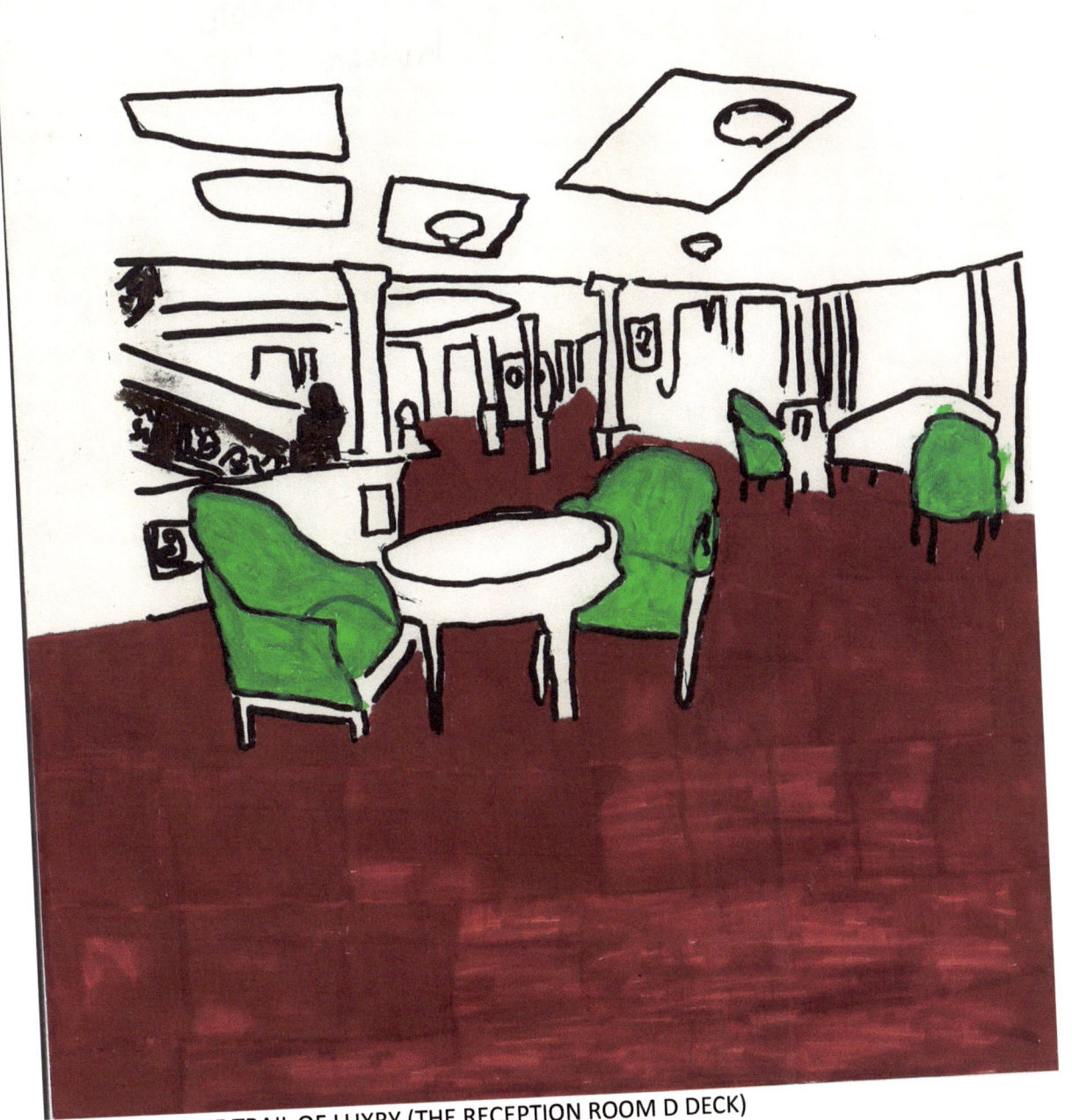

FOLLOWING THE TRAIL OF LUXRY (THE RECEPTION ROOM D DECK)

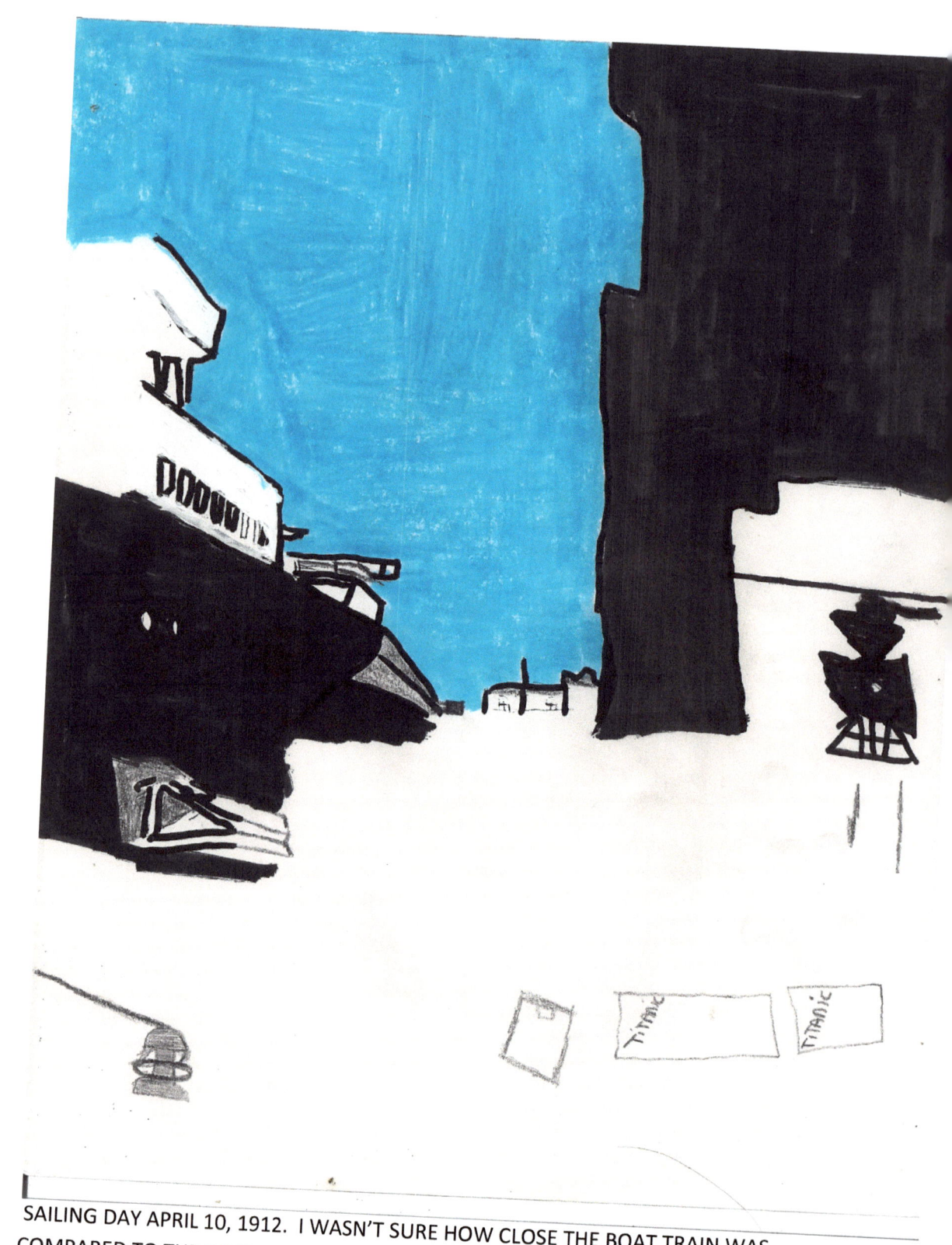

SAILING DAY APRIL 10, 1912. I WASN'T SURE HOW CLOSE THE BOAT TRAIN WAS COMPARED TO THE DOCK SO I PLACED THEM TOGETHER.

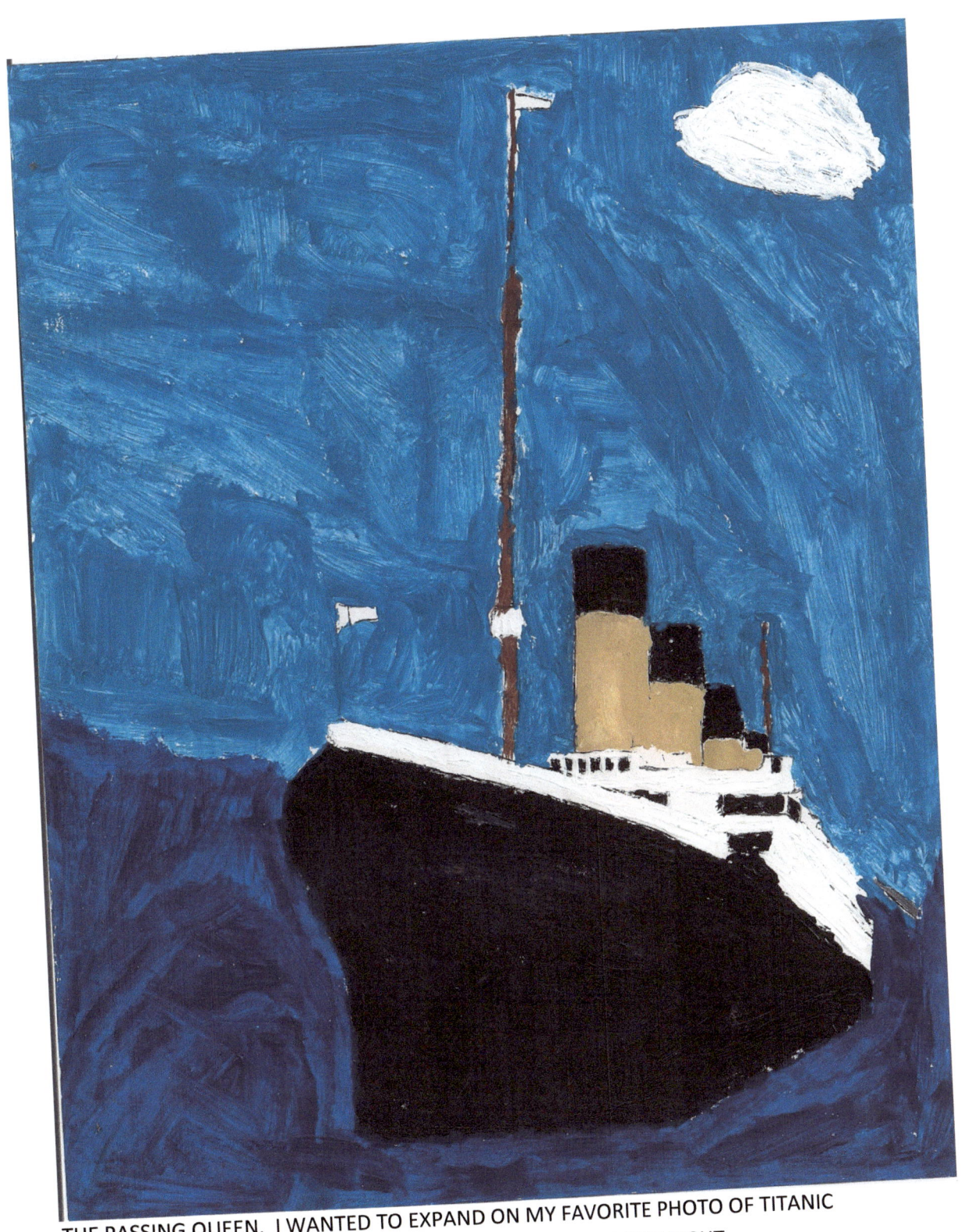

THE PASSING QUEEN. I WANTED TO EXPAND ON MY FAVORITE PHOTO OF TITANIC
LEAVING THE DOCKS THE BERTH IS IN THE BACKGROUND TO THE RIGHT.

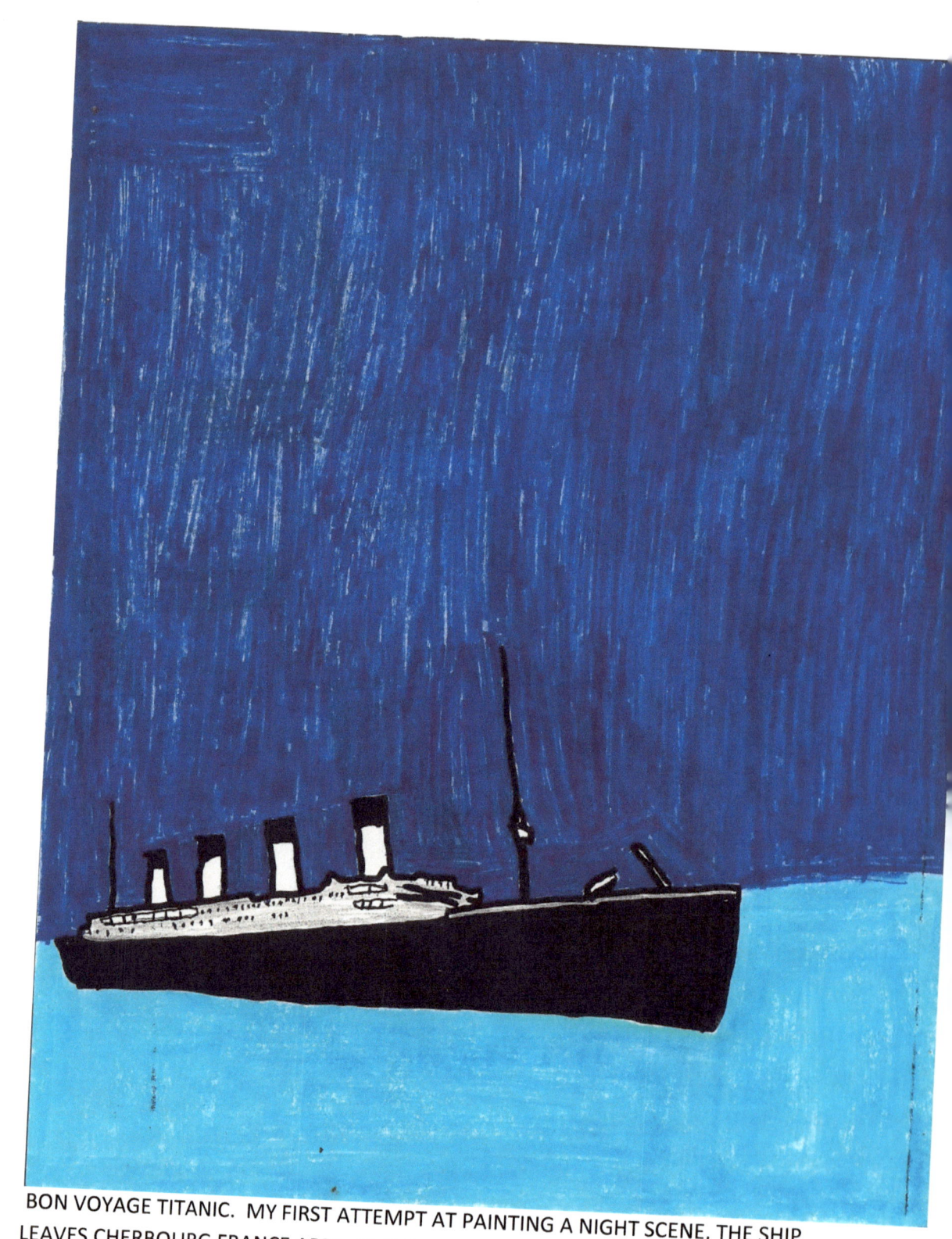

BON VOYAGE TITANIC. MY FIRST ATTEMPT AT PAINTING A NIGHT SCENE, THE SHIP LEAVES CHERBOURG FRANCE APRIL 10 EVENING

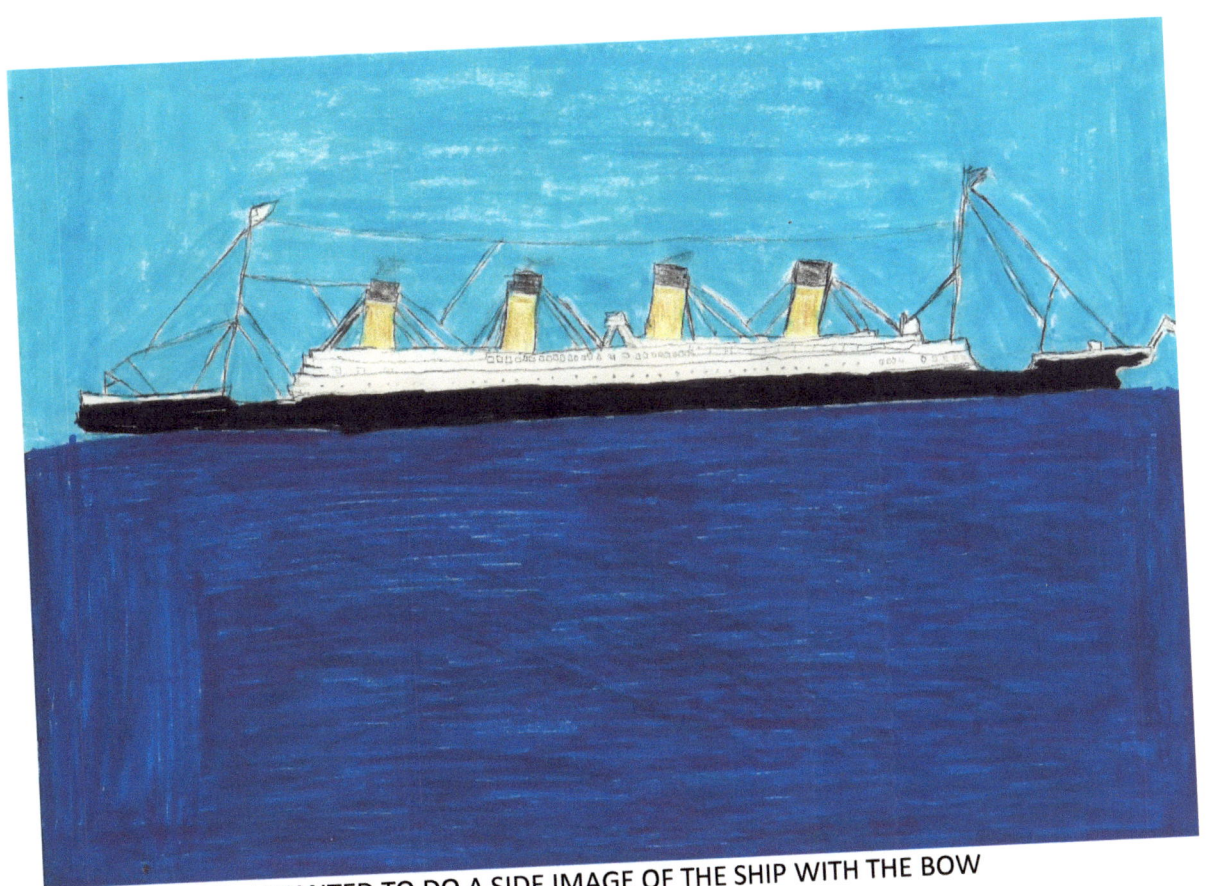

LEAVING COBH. I WANTED TO DO A SIDE IMAGE OF THE SHIP WITH THE BOW
BREAKING WAVES AS THE ENGINES STARTED ON APRIL 11

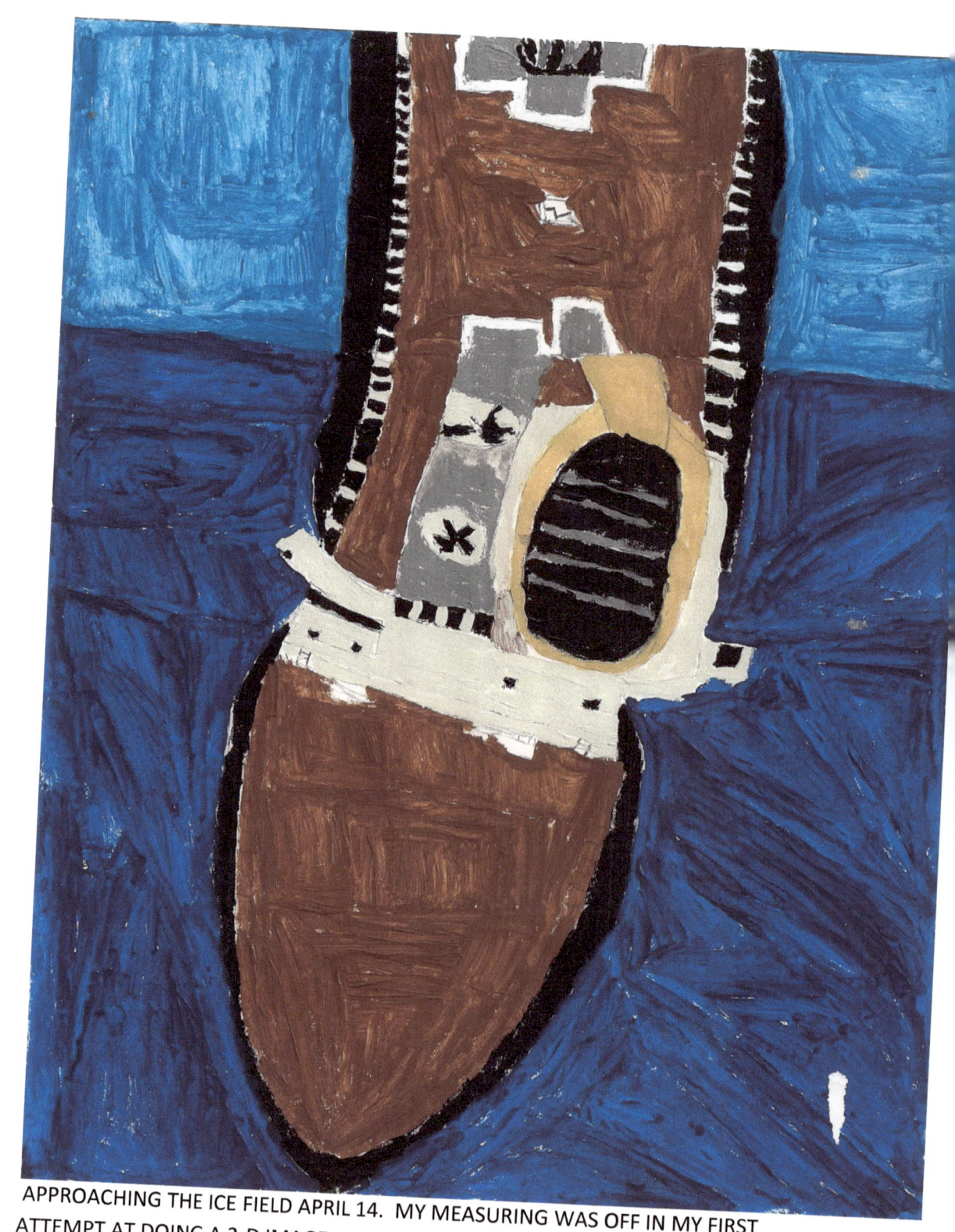

APPROACHING THE ICE FIELD APRIL 14. MY MEASURING WAS OFF IN MY FIRST ATTEMPT AT DOING A 3-D IMAGE.

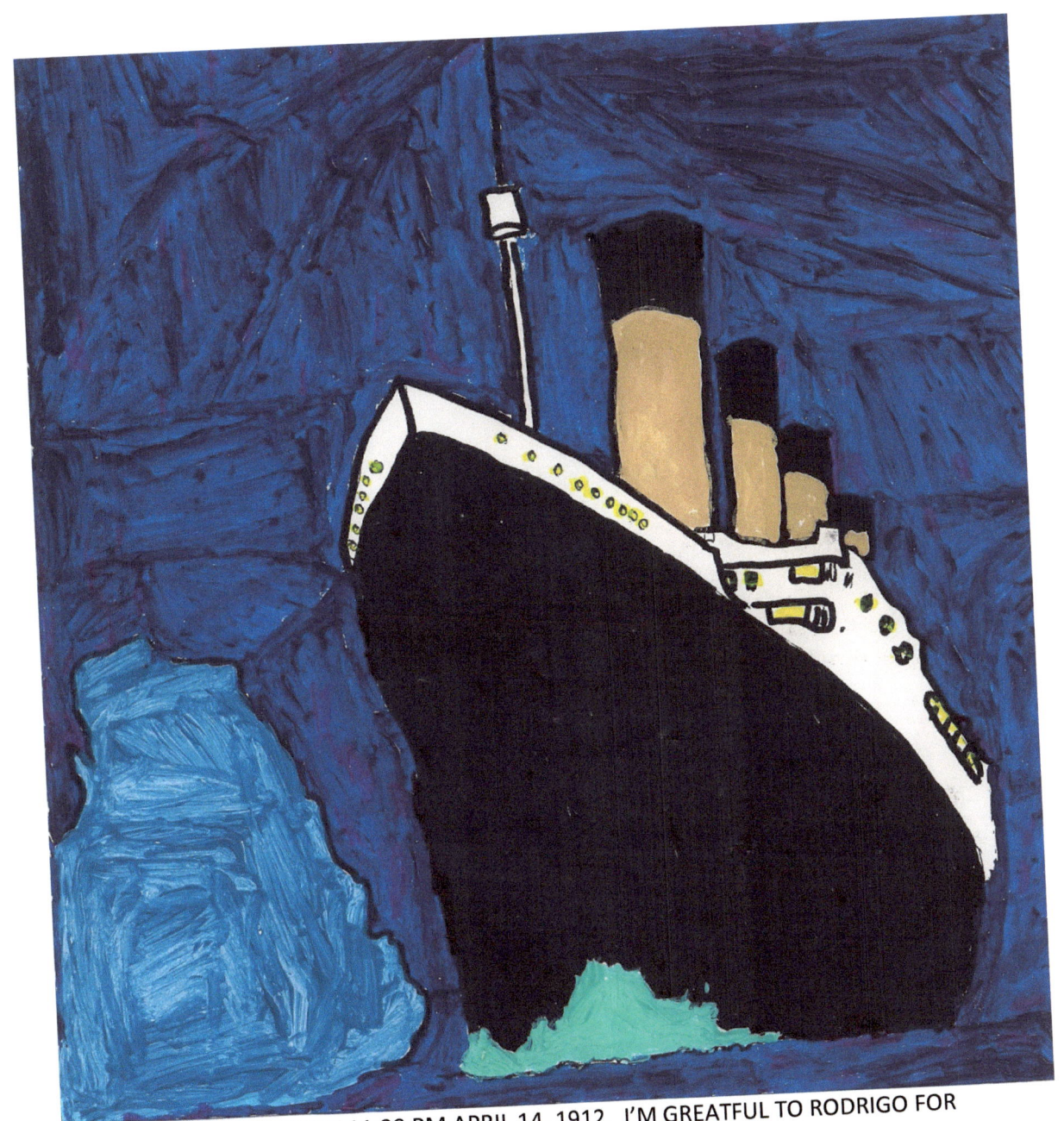

MOMENTS FROM DESTINY 11:39 PM APRIL 14, 1912. I'M GREATFUL TO RODRIGO FOR TEACHING ME HOW TO ADD DEPTH IN AN IMAGE; THIS IS MY PROUDEST PAINTING THAT I'D LATER USE AS A LOGO FOR MY LECTURES.

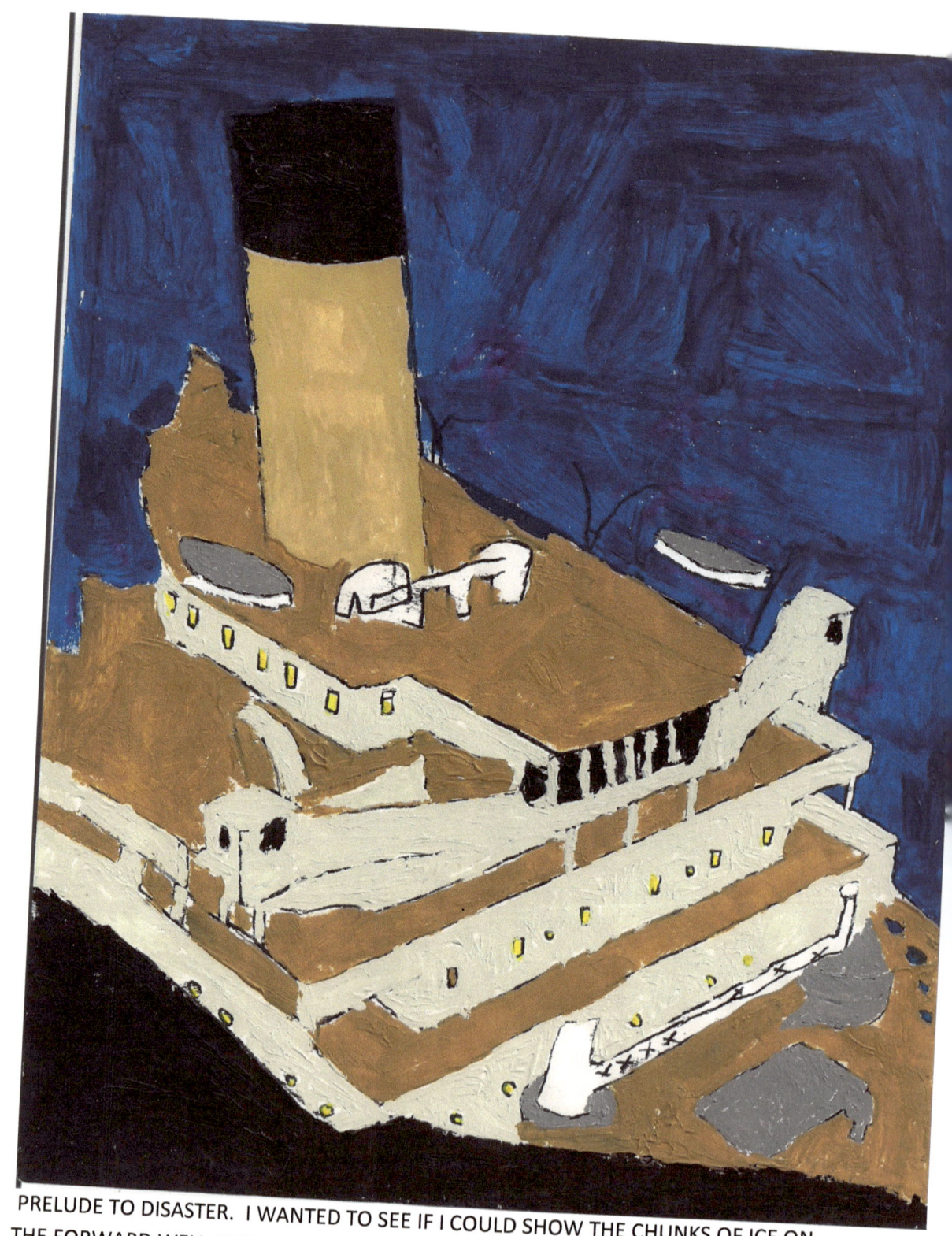

PRELUDE TO DISASTER. I WANTED TO SEE IF I COULD SHOW THE CHUNKS OF ICE ON THE FORWARD WELL DECK.

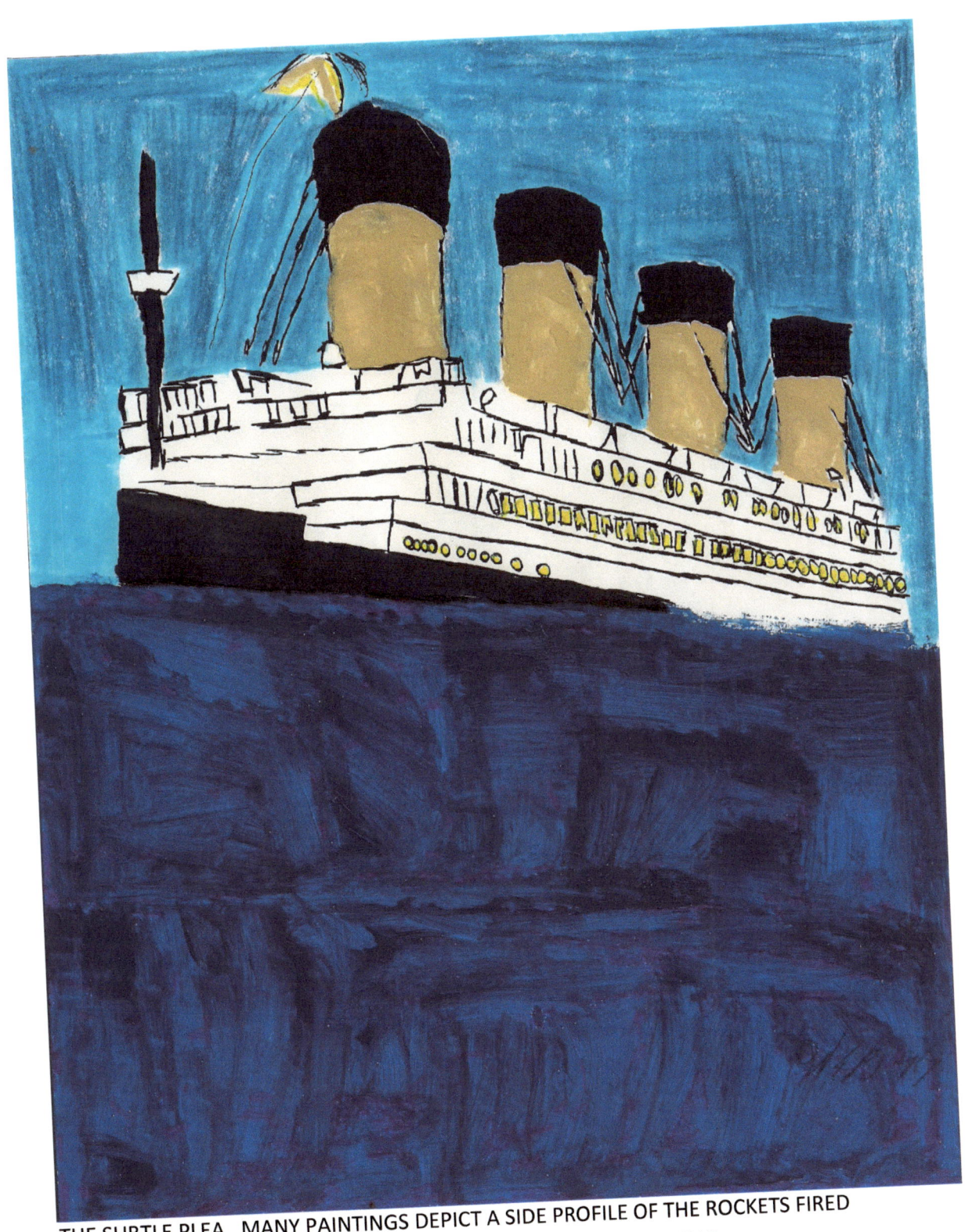

THE SUBTLE PLEA. MANY PAINTINGS DEPICT A SIDE PROFILE OF THE ROCKETS FIRED OFF THE TITANIC I DECIDED TO CHANGE IT INTO A BOW VIEW INSTEAD.

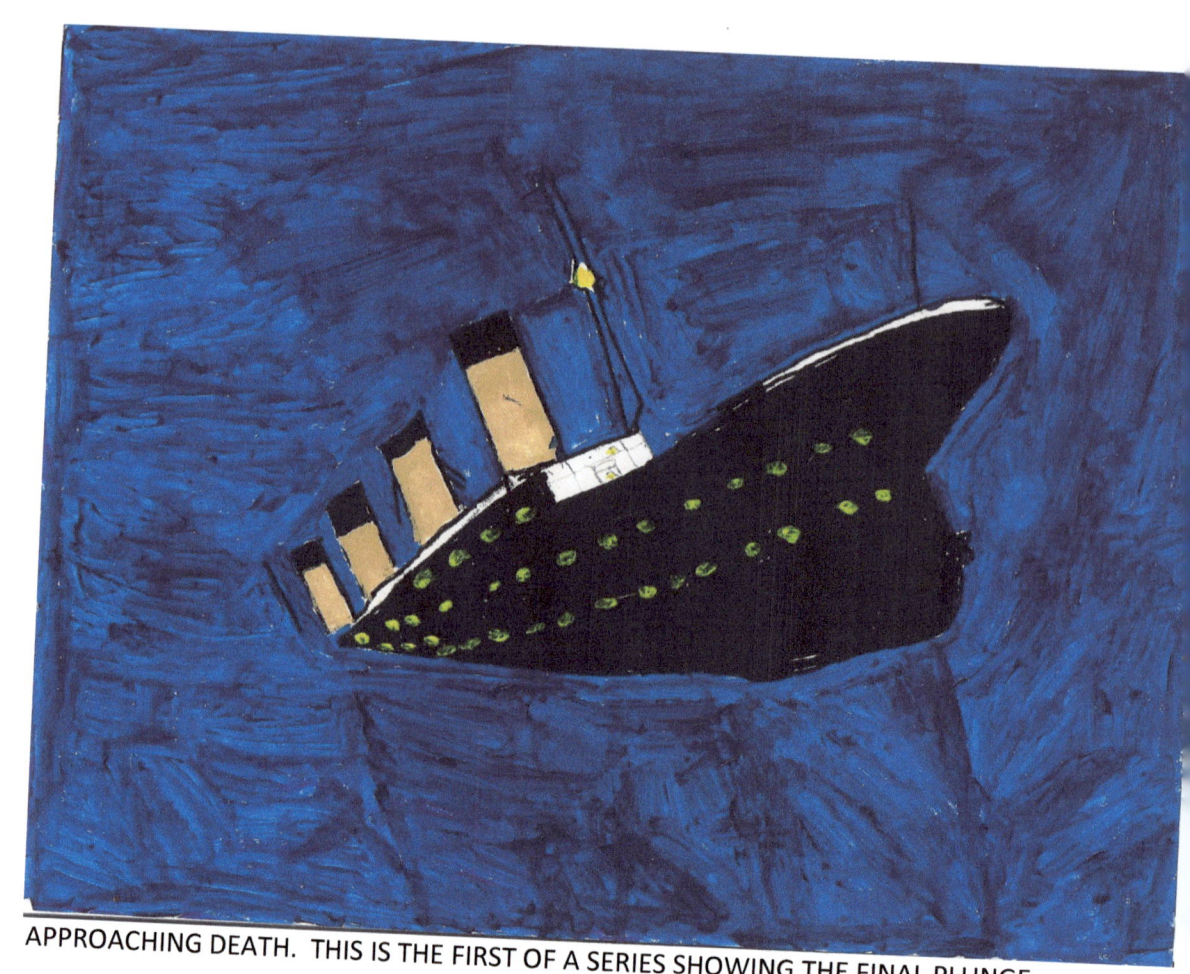

APPROACHING DEATH. THIS IS THE FIRST OF A SERIES SHOWING THE FINAL PLUNGE.

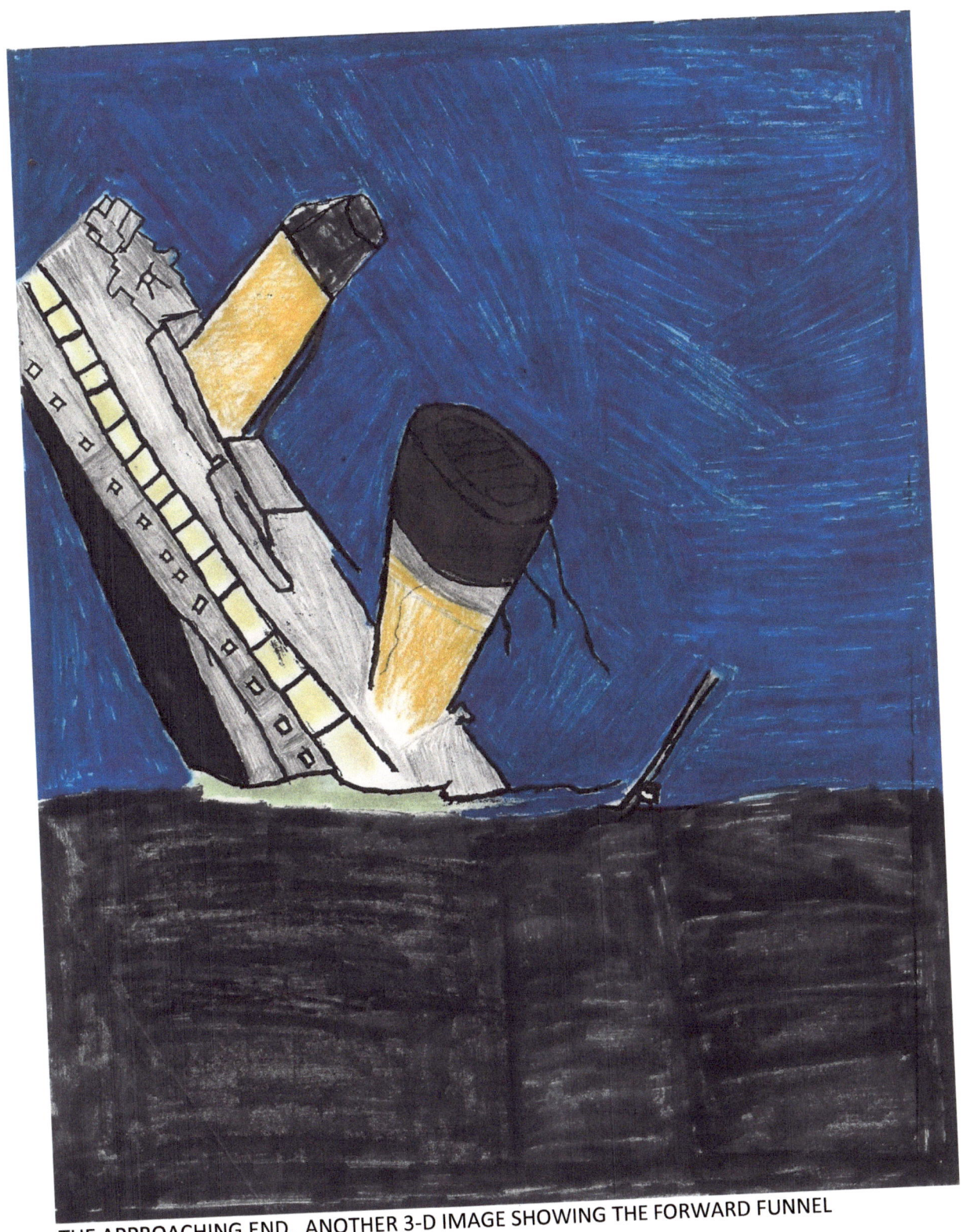

THE APPROACHING END. ANOTHER 3-D IMAGE SHOWING THE FORWARD FUNNEL
COLLAPSING.

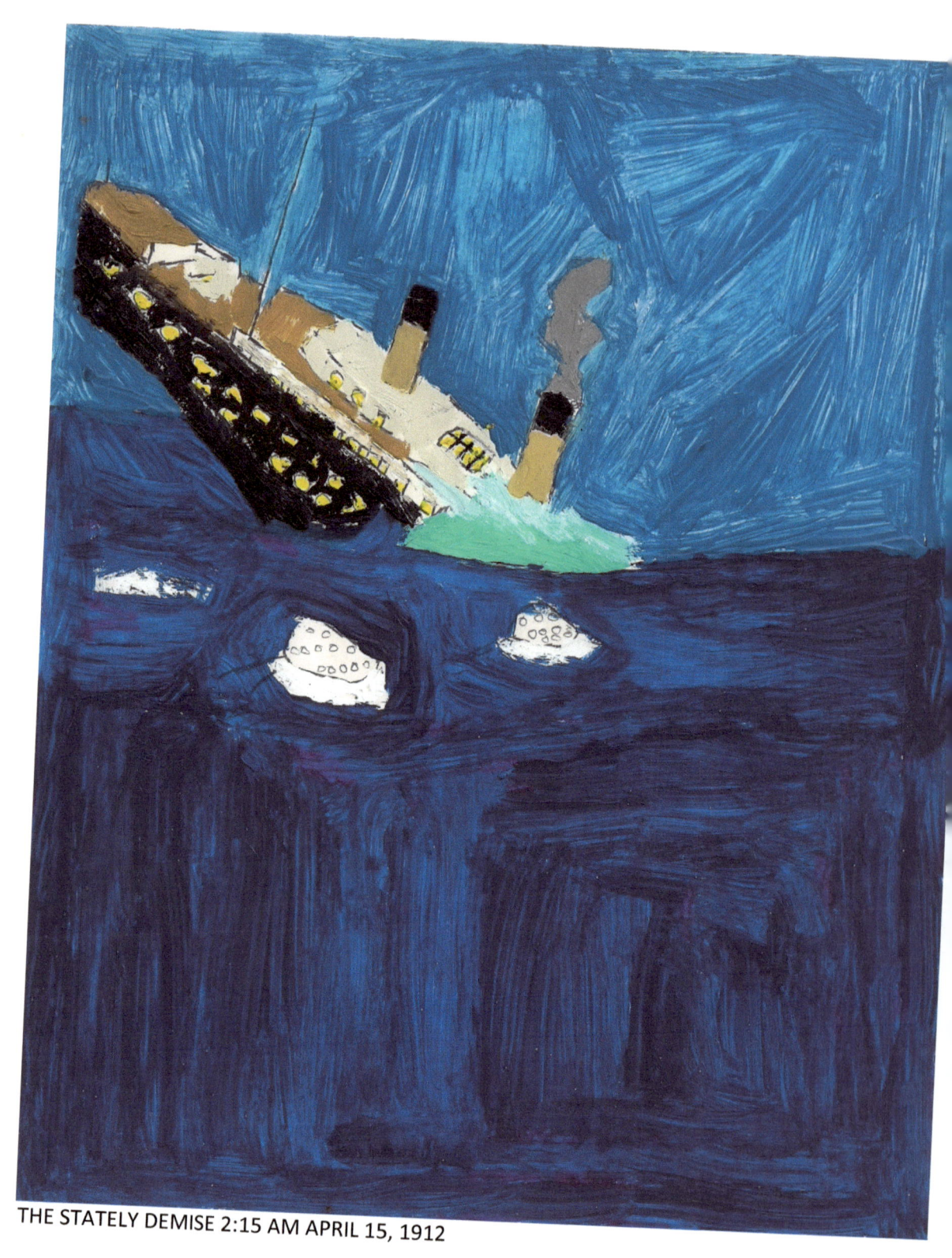

THE STATELY DEMISE 2:15 AM APRIL 15, 1912

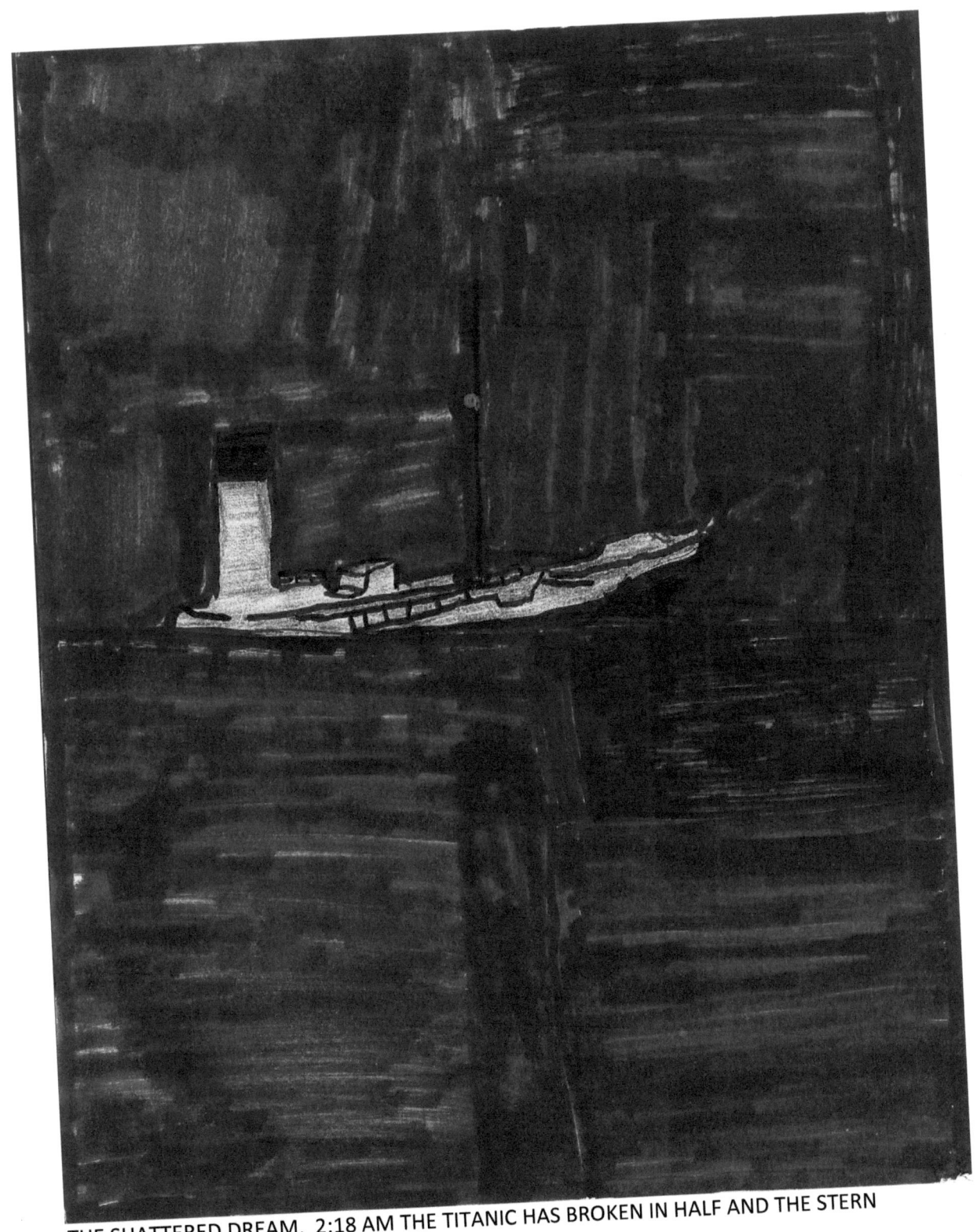

THE SHATTERED DREAM. 2:18 AM THE TITANIC HAS BROKEN IN HALF AND THE STERN SECTION SETTLED ALMOST LEVEL IN THE WATERS.

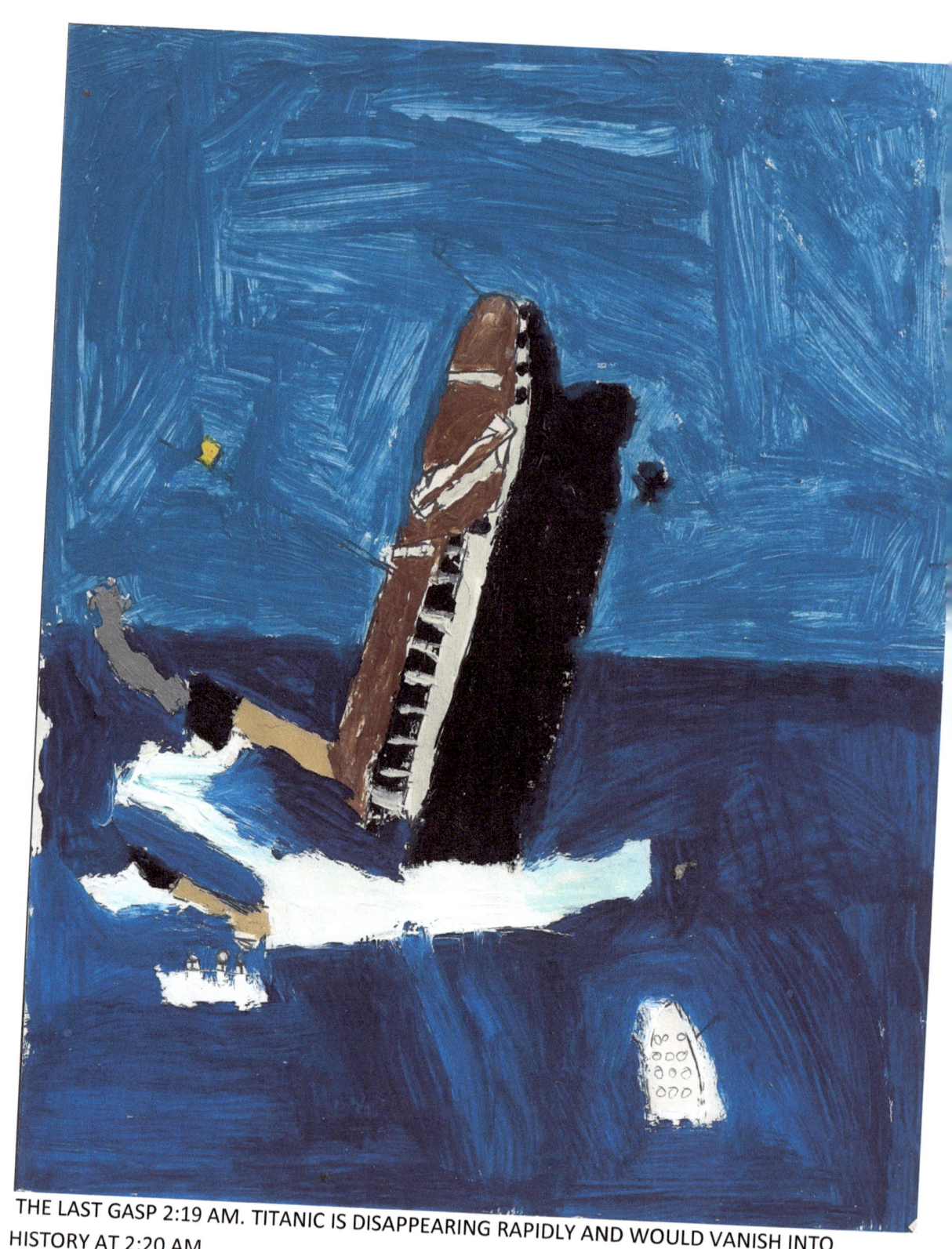

THE LAST GASP 2:19 AM. TITANIC IS DISAPPEARING RAPIDLY AND WOULD VANISH INTO HISTORY AT 2:20 AM.

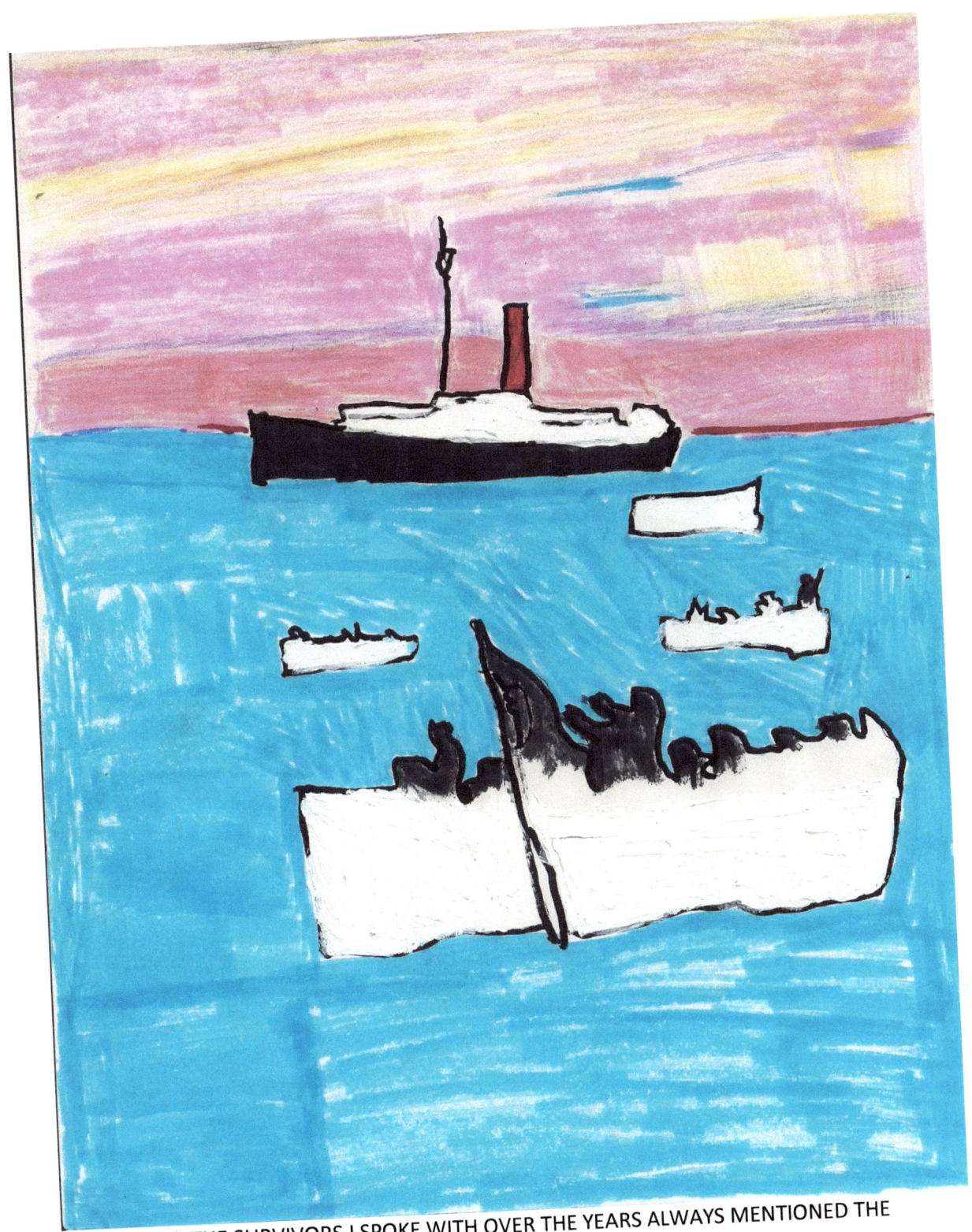

SALVATION! THE SURVIVORS I SPOKE WITH OVER THE YEARS ALWAYS MENTIONED THE CONTRAST OF COLORS IN THE EARLY MORNING AS CARPATHIA CONTINUED THE RESCUE.

A DREAM DESTROYED. ON September 1, 1985 ROBERT BALLARD DISCOVERS THE WRECK OF TITANIC. HER STERN IS SMASHED FROM IMPLOSIONS AND THE DECKS ARE PEELED BACK.

GRACEFUL IN DEATH. COMPARED TO THE STERN HER BOW SITS NEARLY INTACT 2.5 MILES UNDER WATER.

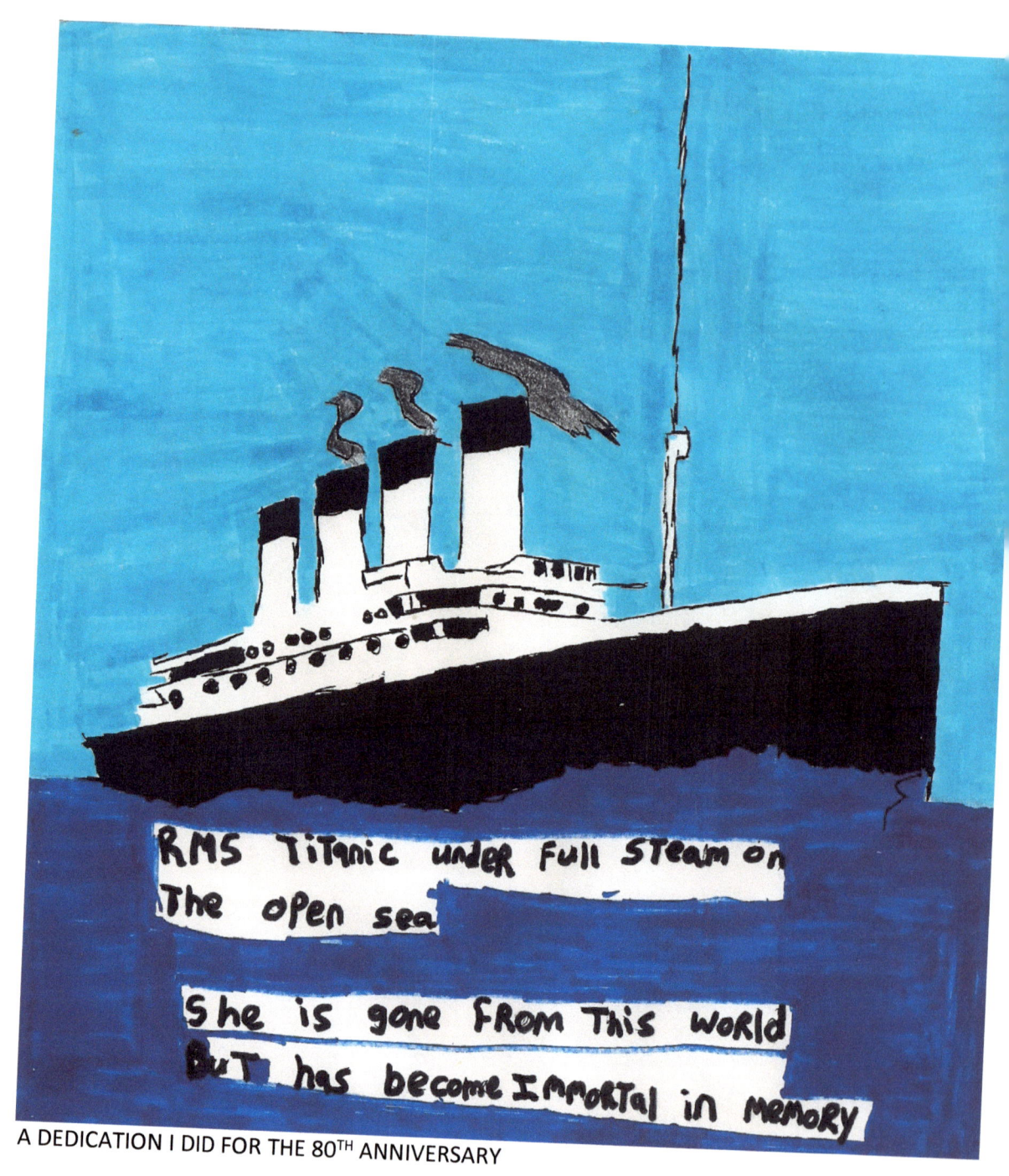

RMS Titanic under full steam on the open sea

She is gone from this world but has become immortal in memory

A DEDICATION I DID FOR THE 80TH ANNIVERSARY

As the US Ambassador to the Titanic Heritage Trust I invite you to become a member and help in preserving the memory of this great ship! Here is what we as a group provide:

The THT is the international charitable trust set up to protect the history and name R.M.S. Titanic and those connected to it. Members receive a copy of "Ocean Times" and can contribute articles as well plus have discounts at THT events.

For more information go to http://www.titanicheritagetrust.org.uk/

OTHER BOOKS BY W.E.BROWER JR.

Confession and True Accounts of the Crazy Clan

Chronicles of the Dragons Bane

The Art and Origins of the Dragons Bane series

Chronicles of the Dragons Bane Volume 2

A Soldier's Journal

The Essays and Wit of W.E. Brower Jr.

Standing In Loves Shadow

Confession and True Accounts of the Crazy Clan revisited

Touched By the Titanic

How to Rearrange Deck Chairs on the Titanic

The Enormously Large Great Big Book of Boobtits Now In 3-D But Not Really!

38th Parallel